GW00498518

Praise for Fiddle Dreams

"John's poetry is imbued with an ever-insightful charm and youthful fascination, much like the man himself."
Declan O'Rourke

"John plays fiddle with joy, sensitivity and humanity. So it's not surprising that his light touch and rhythm sing out in his poetry when he 'fiddles with words'. More power to your elbow, my dear friend."
Ralph McTell

"John's lyrics are like a winged key. They open your mind and then lift you above the mundane. They fly you to June, if in the Northern Hemisphere, or New Year in Patagonia. He's like a non-profit travel agent but always a prophet. For laymen like me he has the key to the pictures."
Damien Dempsey

"Wise, witty, insightful – these poems will uplift you."
Joe Duffy

"John possesses as light a touch with the pen as he does with the bow. He writes with a sense of home and worldliness, at once a gypsy spirit and a pure Dubliner."
Glen Hansard

"Fiddler, poet, creator, dreamer,
Eternally eloquent in demeanor;
Softly spoken, mind alight,
Wistful eyes dance through bushy white;
Words of wonder from pages gleam;
My inspiration … Mr. John Sheahan."
Imelda May

FIDDLE DREAMS

POEMS & LYRICS

DEDALUS PRESS
DUBLIN, IRELAND

for Mary,
Siobhán, Fiachra, Eoin & Ceoladh

THANKS AND ACKNOWLEDGEMENTS

A warm word of thanks to: My family, friends and colleagues for their encouragement and support over the years.

To Ann Egan and Patricia Healy for mothering my early attempts.

To Pat Boran, Seamus Hosey, Tony Curtis, Michael Coady, Dermot Bolger, Gabriel Fitzmaurice, Brendan Kennelly, Theo Dorgan, Paula Meehan, John McNamee, Brendan Graham, Brendan Flynn of *The Clifden Anthology*, Willie Kealy of *The Sunday Independent* and my friends at Listowel Writers Week;

To Ralph McTell, Imelda May, Glen Hansard, Charlie McGettigan, Damien Dempsey and Declan O'Rourke;

To Liam McGrath, Maurice Sweeney and Joe Dolan, of Scratch Films;

To Chris Kavanagh, Imelda Gallagher, Fiach & Ann Ó Broin, Mícheál Ó Caoimh, Phelim Drew, Brian Hand, Jimmy Kelly, Jeannie Bourke, Harriet Roche and Kari Losch.

A number of these poems and lyrics have been performed by the author at concerts, formal and informal, as well as on a variety of RTÉ radio and television programmes over recent years. Poems have previously appeared in print in *The Sunday Independent, The Clifden Anthology* (2013) and in *If Ever You Go: A Map of Dublin in Poetry and Song* (Dedalus Press, 2014). My sincere thanks to the editors and producers for their encouragement and support.

FIDDLE DREAMS

POEMS & LYRICS

John Sheahan

First published in 2015 by
Dedalus Press
13 Moyclare Road
Baldoyle
Dublin 13
Ireland
www.**dedaluspress**.com

Editor: Pat Boran

ISBN 978 1 910251 10 2 (paperback)
ISBN 978 1 910251 13 3 (hardback)

Dedalus Press titles are represented in the UK by
Central Books, 99 Wallis Road, London E9 5LN
and in North America by Syracuse University Press, Inc.,
621 Skytop Road, Suite 110, Syracuse, New York 13244.

Front cover photograph of John Sheahan
copyright © Kathrin Haderer, by permission

The Dedalus Press receives financial assistance from
The Arts Council / An Chomhairle Ealaíon

Contents

❧

FIDDLE DREAMS
Music & Musicians

Soul-Mate 13
Forest Echoes 14
Morning 15
Ronnie's Heaven 16
Evening 18
Sonnet for Luke 19
Sketch of a Dubliner 20
Last Night's Fun... 22
Luke ... 21st Anniversary 23
Stray Music 24
Liam Clancy 25
Fiddle Dream 26
Time Gentlemen, Please 27
Colour Soundings 28
A Tune for Every Season 29
Uncle Jimmy Murders 'Danny Boy' 30
Awkward Silence 31
Banjo Barney 32
Remembering Ciarán 34
Marino Air 36
The Long Note 37
Sound Man Tom 38
Symphony for Woodwind 40
Partnership 42
Eamon Keane at the NCH 43
The Busker 44
Luke's Gravestone 45
Grace Note 46

GOING TO THE WELL
Family & Friends

Quiet Wisdom 49
Spirit Brother 50
Going to the Well 51
Forgotten Rhymes 52
My Father 55
Auntie Peggy 56
To Sadhbh with Love 57
To Croíadh at Six Months 58
A Glimpse of My Father 59
Dabble Day 60
Seventh Anniversary 62
Soul Search 63
Timeless Clay 64
The Turf Cutter 65
Dreamtime 66
Woodsman 67

SWEEPINGS OF THE WORKSHOP
Art & Craft

The Chimney Sweep 71
Behan's 'Children of Lir' 72
Wood Carver 73
Wood Shavings 74
The Solidity of Matter 75
The Fiddle Maker's Workshop 76
Sweepings of the Workshop 77

SIGNATURES IN AIR
Times & Places

The Monthly Clip 81
Out of Bounds 83
Countdown 85
Silent Preacher 86
Confession 87
Connemara 88
Trom agus Éadrom 89
Sunflowers 90
Autumn 91
Wheatfield Table 92
Tree Seasons 93
Stereo Tracks 94
Signature 95

❧

ABOUT THE AUTHOR 96

Fiddle Dreams

Music & Musicians

Soul-Mate

Your fingers tease out feelings from my soul.
Your hands caress my slender neck
And stroke my long white hair.

You hold me snugly to your breast,
Hungry for the food of love,
And gaze upon my shapely form –
My bosom, white with fairy dust.

You shelter me from daily harm
And nightly wrap me from the cold.
You seek me in the morning light,
Forever shadowing my soul.

Guardian of angelic sounds,
Come play with me ...

Forest Echoes

I sense a forest in my fiddle,
Ghosts of trees beneath my chin,
Belly and back of spruce and maple;
On fingered ebony a bird sings.

I sense the terror of the axe,
Slow-motion fall of timber,
Phantom pain of tree stump,
Renewal of green shoots, under.

I draw my bow ... A white-tailed horse
Goes galloping back where time has flown.
Through fertile ground he sets a course,
To find where seeds of sound were sown.

Rider – blur of wind-blown tunes –
Circles the forest round and round.
To ghosts of fallen trees, a nod;
To spruce and maple, the gift of sound.

I rest my bow, the reins fall slack,
My tunes are stalled within a riddle.
From leaf and branch I lure them back.
I sense a forest in my fiddle.

Morning

Untouched ebony,
Mute strings yearn for rosined bow –
The lonely fiddle.

Ronnie's Heaven

What's it like, Ronnie – your new life?
Is it the way the old masters painted it –
Floating on a damp cloud
In the company of winged creatures
Listening to non-stop harp music?

I could paint you in,
But not your expectations:
"Would somebody for Christ's sake
Get me down from here and show me
The fountain of champagne – I thought this
Was meant to be a celebration!"

I'll paint a different picture instead:
I see your spirit, freed at last
From earthly shackles,
Soaring to a new consciousness –
Communicating with Kavanagh
Without the encumbrance of words,
Without the embarrassment of being barred
From four Baggot Street pubs ...

All is clear now ...
Ulysses simpler than the Lord's Prayer,
Beckett no longer waiting for Godot,
And Joe Ó Broin sidling over
With an impish grin:
"How're ya, Ronnie, you brought me fame at last.
I heard Cliodhna and Phelim picked me poem
For the end of your mass,
But you needn't have hurried ...

There's no closing time up here –
Just one continuous holy hour."
Now Deirdre comes into focus,
Bridging and healing a painful absence.

Unhindered by bodies,
Your spirits embrace and entwine
In a never-ending spiral of joy,

Leaving behind the three
Great imponderables that tortured you:
"What is life?"
"What is art?"
And "Where the fuck is Barney?"

Ronnie Drew, 1934 – 2008

Evening

I am a cry of creation,
Chant of children at play,
Jingle of pennies in a pocket,
Creak of an idle gate.

I am a whisper of spring,
Summer drone of bees,
Leafy lament of autumn,
Whistle of winter through trees.

When faces blur in the dance,
I am the shuffle of shoes.
When horns honk in the night
I am the sound of the blues.

Sonnet for Luke

A fiery halo crowns your lived-in face.
You shine forth like a beacon from the throng;
Among your fellow peers you set the pace,
And hush the gathered crowd with your song.

Committed to the cause of human rights,
You hold aloft the flame of Amnesty;
When striking workers seek you in their plight,
You rally to their cause unstintingly.

A minstrel boy, you charm your way through life,
Enriching all who chance to pass your way;
You shelter wayward spirits from the night,
And keep them plied with drink till dawn of day.

Though links with us alas too soon are severed,
Your spirit and your song will live forever.

Sketch of a Dubliner

Bearded bass boom,
Slim-lined,
Short-fused,
Razor-sharp.

Centre-stage
Holding forth;
Centre-bar
Toasting life.

Purveyor of street ballad,
Crafter of story-line,
Disciple of Zozimus,
Flirting with fame.

Imbiber of the black stuff,
Epicentre of the craic,
Master of retort
Outwitting the heckler.

Jovial raconteur
Conjuring with words,
Precision timing,
Knock-out punch line.

Grumpy at morning,
Barbed wire vinegar;
Convivial at evening,
Rose without thorns.

Champion of the underdog
Dethroning the haughty,
Sounding uncomfortable truths,
Uplifting the needy

Disenchanted,
Weary of applause,
Wary of patronage,
Impatient for the encore.

Distillation of the Liffey,
Salt of the earth,
Dublin personified –
Ronnie Drew.

Last Night's Fun

for Seamus Begley

Begley, in harness ...
Stretching and squeezing
A box of air
Into pleated rainbows,
Fanning us aflame
With slides and polkas.

Drawn by your magnetic field,
A *meitheal* of musicians
Gathers in a swirl
Of wind and strings.

Powered by bellows,
Fuelled by a Dingle gale,
You dance us dizzy
Till faces blur
And sparks rise off the floor.

When the storm abates,
You lure us *cois tine,*
Weaving a tapestry of
Sean-nós, myth and legend,
Till dawn breaks the spell
And daylight reclaims us.

In the stillness of morning
Ghosts of unplayed tunes
Linger in the bellows,
Impatient for the kiss of life.

Luke ... 21st Anniversary

2005

You've come of age in death,
Keeper of a golden key;
Forever young, since you
Abandoned time,
While we've aged visibly.

We linger in your shadow,
While you have risen
To a new consciousness
Where music is imagined, and words
Are scattered among the stars.

Stray Music

In a vision, at the waking edge of sleep, I fiddle,
Committing to memory stray music that finds me,
Till dawn comes, and a scattering of notes takes flight.

Casting a tune-maker's net, I lure them back,
Quavers and crotchets on fresh manuscript.
My fiddle breaks the silence.

Liam Clancy

Memories of an Irish Troubadour

Liam, of poetic eye
And wistful phrase,
Sketching for us your youth,
Your halcyon days,

From faltering steps through Carrick,
To New World schemes,
Luring our spirits westward,
To visit your dreams

Of life and love and art
And music's magic spell;
Unveiling silent songs of youth
Their ancient tales to tell.

Treading the boards on Broadway,
Part-time wandering star,
Apprenticed to philosophers
In Greenwich Village bars.

Poised between the two great mysteries,
Cast in life's unfolding play,
Content until the Master Playwright
Calls you back to clay.

Fiddle Dream

Countless miles mapped
On scuffed canvas cover;
Inside, sleeping fiddle, snug in velvet,
Reeling in the years ...

Endless ribbon of road
Winding back through humid nights
In half-remembered places,
Blurred montage of halls and smokey clubs
And after-hours in nameless pubs
Where clocks have stopped.

Rambling nights in lost shebeens
Where jigs and reels come sloping in
With mountainy men in overcoats and caps,
A feast of fiddlers in wild abandon
Throwing whiskey-flavoured tunes
To a blur of wheeling dancers.

Rattling of heels on flagstones,
Heartbeat boom of bodhrán,
Whistle and flute competing for air,
Wheezy squeezebox stretched to the limit,

Dreaming fiddle,
White with rosin dust.

Time Gentlemen, Please

i.m. Seamus Ennis

I dive into a surge of churning triplets and grace notes
And levitate on a sudden updraught from a piper's bellows,
Pinning me to the dark smokey ceiling of O'Donoghue's Pub.

Oblivious of my plight,
The session continues below, in relentless pursuit
Of nameless, never-ending jigs and reels.

Years pass and the music fades, as one by one
The ageing musicians spiral up to share my fate,
Leaving behind a motley menagerie of bodhrán players.

Blissfully unaware that the music has ended,
They continue, like a plague, in a cacophony of
Contradictory rhythms that show no hint of mercy.

Has my worst nightmare become a reality?
Am I doomed to endure this torture forever?
Above me, I hear the distant sound of harp music!

Colour Soundings

If orange and green were sound
Instead of colour,
We'd hearken to the echo
Of fierce cacophony.

In these enlightened days,
We retune ourselves
To subtle shades
Of deeper harmony.

Let's orchestrate
The coloured sounds
Of fiddle, fife and drum,
In a brave and lasting symphony.

A Tune for Every Season

after Vivaldi

You listened
With angels' ears
To seasonal wisps
Of stray music:

Stuttering joy of songbird,
Hushed whisper of waving corn,
Rustling lament of fallen leaf,
Silence of snow.

When your treasury of sound
Was gathered,
When every mood was matched,
You floated home

On rising strings,
Triumphal brass,
Sombre woodwind,
Thunder of timpani,

Stirring the air
In remembered rhythm,
Echoing the moods
That gifted you …

A tune for every season.

Uncle Jimmy Murders 'Danny Boy'

At the mere mention of his party piece,
Uncle Jimmy takes the floor.
With scant regard for crotchet or quaver,
He is airborne with *Danny Boy*.

Free as a banshee on the wing,
He takes wild swipes at the melody,
Blissfully out-soaring it on ascending passages,
Swooping unashamedly towards the bass clef
On reckless descents.

Goaded on by the glee of the mocking crowd,
He throws Caruso-shapes to an imagined gallery.
On full throttle for the challenge of the upper octave,
He overshoots his target by a delightful semitone.

Oblivious of the trail of music-debris in his wake,
He braces himself for the final assault –
Strangling *Danny Boy,* note by note,
As he soars into the stratosphere
For a glorious crescendo.

Awkward Silence

In the pause between
Movements of a symphony ...
Counterfeited calm;

Reservoir of applause
Threatening the dam.

Banjo Barney

Your plectrum, a fledgling bird;
Squeezed too tightly, it chokes;
Too lightly, it flies away.

Cosy in your care,
It nests between finger and thumb,
Heeding your touch
To wake wonders on string.

Dancing fingers paint pictures in air,
Barneyisms embellish the craic,
And your love song steals the limelight.

In tune with yourself
Jigging for mackerel,
Wind-song in the rigging,
Rhythm of rolling wave.

Heave and haul of shanty,
Audience lashed with salty foam,
You, on the quarter deck,
Guide us round the dreaded Horn.

Without fuss or warning
You heed a whispered call;
Adrift in the doldrums,
You succumb to the long sleep.

Your hands, fixed in death,
Your fledgling bird now flown.
Your cap, tilted to the north star,

Your sails, rigged for a far horizon,
Heave away, haul away,
Sail away to the music of silence.

Barney McKenna, 1939 – 2012

Remembering Ciarán

Ciarán Bourke, 1935 – 1988

Long-haired, wayward chieftain
Sloping in from Celtic mist,
Recycling myth and legend
Through the holes
Of a battered tin whistle.

Desk-bound harness untackled,
You surrendered to the lure of living.
Like a moth to a flame, you followed
The warm glow of music and the craic.

Bhí an Ghaeilge agat ón gcliabhán, *
Beguiling *Peggy Lettermore,*
Lamenting *Eanach Cuain;*
Embroidering and stitching
Your story to the night air
With guitar and harmonica.

In old shebeens where time was barred,
You toasted life with *Preab San Ól.*
Whiskey-flavoured yarns flowed and
Meandered from byways of memory
Till dawn broke the spell
Through a smokey haze.

"Well that ties a knot on that one,"
You'd say, saluting the dawn
And the gift of another day.

When fate struck a cruel blow,
You bore your lot with stoic acceptance.
With shepherd's crook, your footsteps
Found their echo in half-remembered places,
Till they faded, all too soon,
Back to the shadows of a Celtic twilight.

You had Irish from the cradle

Marino Air

for Siobhán

Idly plucking harp strings,
I tease from the air a secret-in-waiting –
A tune in search of a voice.

Mysteriously stirred,
I unravel time and tone
To cradle them in silent symbols.

Black dots on a white page,
They stir remembered rhythms,
And I waltz again with Marino air.

The Long Note

You were the one for the phrasing, Luke.
I loved the way you played hide-and-seek
With the pulse of a song,

Stretching a note beyond the bar line,
'Til you left us dangling at a cliff edge.

With the thread about to snap,
You rescued the rhythm and reeled us in
To catch a missing heart beat.

Sound Man Tom

for Tom O'Brien

Sound man Tom,
Makin' small sounds bigger,
Makin' quiet sound louder,
Makin' thin sounds thicker.

Sound man Tom,
Sure you've grown up with sound,
Must be all in your head
Just goin' round and round.

It just had to break out
With your wit and your timin',
Sure sooner or later
I knew you'd be rhymin'.

You'll be timid at first
And then, I will warrant,
What began as a trickle
Will build up to a torrent.

On the next UK tour
When the boys go for *wets,*
Sure yourself and meself
Will do poetic duets.

When the cables are spooled
And the gear's stowed away
Sure we'll tangle with words
Till the breakin' of day.

And when mornin' comes round
And for breakfast we go
Sure we'll slag one and all
With our own rhyming show.

We'll hide Paddy's scotch
And put him on the rocks
On top of Croagh Patrick
For a month to detox.

We'll give Eamonn a year
To learn Irish in Connaught,
And the first thing he'll say
Will be *Slán agus Beannacht*.

We'll give Seán a new ministry
With the gaeltacht his goal,
To abolish the *sean-nós*
And revive rock and roll.

We'll get Barney a grammy
For his banjo ability,
If he ever comes back
From the sea of tranquillity.

So sound man Tom,
We'll write many a riddle
With you on the knobs
And meself on the fiddle.

But we'd never use rhymin'
To offend or expose,
We'll just mind our own business
Of buttons and bows.

Symphony for Woodwind

Orchestra of trees;
Symphony for woodwind;
The great oak nods to the breeze –
Let the music begin!

Light rustle of leafy cymbals
Wafting in the overture;
Breezes twisting, slanting, shifting,
Testing every aperture.

Below, the drone of bass bassoon
Curving round each bough and bark;
Above, the air in octaves rising,
Swirling through the tall windharp.

Uncarved oboes, clarinets, flutes –
Solid, silent, tree trunk-bound,
Awaken to their nature's calling,
Yearning to augment the sound.

Windswept drumsticks beat the bough,
Gusty rhythms guide the tune;
Timpani of thunder rolling,
Spotlit by a harvest moon.

Daylight wakes her feathered songsters,
Wings and wind in harmony,
Assembling for the dawning chorus,
Crowning nature's symphony.

Morning lifts her veil of dawn,
Sleepy saplings sigh and sway;
Gentle wisps of music linger,
Weeping willows waltz away.

Partnership

Competing for supremacy
Fiddle and bow were at it hammer and tongs;
"Consider my flawless pedigree," said the fiddle,
"My fine body of spruce and maple,
Delicately carved scroll, uniquely shaped f-holes,
And, above all, my true harmonics and exquisite tone."

The bow tossed back a shock of white horsehair,
Arched its spring spine and replied:
"You are indeed a perfect specimen of fiddle-hood,
But without me you would be doomed
To a sentence of silence, save for the lonely sound
Of pizzicato and the wind.
What then of your fine pedigree?"

"And what of yours?" countered the fiddle.
"What music can you boast of?
You may flex and flaunt your pernambuco body,
But without me you would never have risen
Above the sound of a horse's fart!"

Suitably humbled, the bow sulked
While the fiddle reflected
On the truth of the bow's reproach.
Dumb silence reigned till they acquiesced,
Acknowledging interdependence.

With renewed regard for complementary talents
They surrendered to the maestro's touch,
Restored to their natural calling
In a marriage of music, time and wood.

Eamon Keane at the NCH

Steinway lid agape,
Eamon settles, assumes posture,
Eyes closed, soul-sounding.

Solitary note casts a spell,
Shyly lingers, rejoices in its own potential –
Stepping stone to other-worldliness.

Led by a swirl of fingers,
A kaleidoscope of butterflies claims the air,
Trading colour for sound.

In flights of fancy, notes spin out of orbit,
Collide and merge in a seamless world of birdsong,
Twinkling stars, cascading waterfalls.

Familiar refrains deftly disguised
Within a flurry of flattened fifths and added ninths
Slowly slip the mask for short-lived identity,

Then resume camouflage in playful parody.
Mozart twinkles in the night sky;
Beethoven is at home with three blind mice.

With spirits lifted,
We dwell in a Salley Garden
Somewhere over the rainbow.

The Busker

When the wandering fiddler busked the Ha'penny Bridge
His music wove a spell that stirred the heart.
Free-born notes, transcending written music,
Reached out and touched the souls of all who passed.

His grip upon the bow defied convention,
And, likewise, the fiddle's tilted slope.
His wrist embraced the neck in first position,
Yet music soared, though all the rules he broke.

Held in awe by many schooled in music,
They tried in vain to analyse his art,
But a hidden depth escaped their shallow probing:
The well from whence his music sprung – his heart.

Luke's Gravestone

Cold as the wind
That carried your ghost.

Silent as the songs
That remain unsung.

Lonely as an echo
From the Jail of Cluain Meala.

Solitary as your silhouette
Going home by railings
After closing time.

Upright and defiant as your stance
When you challenged the puppets of power:
'For What Died the Sons of Róisín?'

Like your voice …
Unweathered by time
This granite gravestone.

Your epitaph – a simple claim;
Between the two great mysteries,
Your place, your name.

LUKE KELLY
DUBLINER
1940 – 1984

Grace Note

Enchantress of a tune,
You charm a note with a kiss
From the gods. The spirit leaps
And you are gone.

Going to the Well

Family & Friends

Quiet Wisdom

for Uncle Jim

"Have you travelled much, Uncle Jim?"
"I was in Dublin once for a match,"
He said proudly with a grin.
"An All-Ireland Final, in Croke Park."

"And I stayed in Murphy's B&B
In Jones's Road.
I suppose you know Mrs. Murphy,"
He remarked.

I smiled an inner secret smile.
How innocent, how limited,
How untravelled, I thought.
And then I saw myself unravel.

I can't milk a cow, or plough a furrow,
Or tell when corn is ripe for scythe,
Or tell a robin from a sparrow,
Or tell which songbird sings on high,
Or tell the elm from the ash
Or tell the weather from the signs
Known to the farmer.

But *he* can!

Now I learn from his quiet wisdom
In his university of fields.

Spirit Brother

for Denis

In mother's misty eyes
I glimpsed your fledgling soul –
The image of my brother, Denis,
Your earthly half-twin.

When you strayed with angels
Your name was saved
And gifted to me.
I warm your vacant space,
Shape your unformed signature,
Awaken your dormant melody.

When shades of evening gather,
You are the half-light
Of Denis's shadow;
Unsung harmony of his song;
Silent couplet of his sonnet.

Spirit brother,
Your familiar absence lingers.
Infant angel,
You grow to fill our heart-space.

Going to the Well

with Uncle Jimmy

Your giant stride leads the way;
Idle swing of empty buckets
Creaking rusty music;
My tin gallon cans in harmony.

Ancient stepping stones across the field ...
Scattered notes of a lost tune
Waiting for a dancer ...
My nimble feet match their random rhythm
To a well of wonder.

Window into the ground,
Sky looking up,
Tilted vessels swallow their shadows
In gulps.

Brimming buckets buckle and belly,
Heaving sighs of metal fatigue;
Sundance on restless ripples ...
Dappled gold on cheek and chin ...

We straighten to balance our burden –
Scales of justice zig-zagging homeward;
Twin trails of silver jewels, our signatures,
Glistening through the summer dust.

Forgotten Rhymes

Skippin' ropes turnin',
Kids in a line
Chantin' out the rhythms,
Skippin' to the rhymes.

Hop scotch, piggy beds,
Squares in a row,
Step on a line
And out you go!

Playin' hide-and-seek,
Who's on?
All close your eyes –
I'm gone!

Found a secret place,
Never find me here!
Oh Janey! I hear them comin',
Gettin' awful near!

Collectin' marbles,
Wheeler-dealer,
Six glass ones
For your steeler.

Dandelion flowers,
Every kid's dread,
Pick one up,
You'll piss in the bed!

Do you like butter?
Yes or no?
Kids can tell!
Buttercup glow!

Saturday pics,
Follyin' upper,
Home for tea,
Chips for supper.

Croker on Sunday,
All folly Heffo,
His army's goin' to win
And that's for deffo!

Orchards ripe,
In for the raid,
Gansey full of apples,
Now who's afraid?

Comic swappin',
Money scanty,
Two old *Beanos*
For this week's *Dandy!*

Early from school,
Caught in the kitchen!
No eker to do?
You've gotta be mitchin'!

Autumn comin',
Conker spree,
A golden horde
From the chestnut tree.

A hole with a nail
And a piece of twine,
My one's harder!
You won't conquer mine!

Christmas is comin',
The goose is gettin' fat,
Just can't remember now!
We'd a rhyme for that!

Innocent games,
Precious times,
Fadin' away
Like forgotten rhymes.

My Father

I see you now …
A rural exile
In an urban garden,

Your broad back bent
To the spade, renewing your
Acquaintance with the soil.

I see well-worn tools
That knew your father's hands,
Coaxing clods of unwilling clay.

You are a giant
Peeling off the world's overcoat,
And I, a child of the city,
Discovering worms.

Auntie Peggy

Your 87th birthday party,
And you are back to your old ways,
Favouring me surreptitiously
With tasty morsels from your plate.

Your furtive glance
Cautions me:
"Not a word to the others."
Your guarded wink seals my lips.

In your presence
In this silent ritual
I am a boy again.

Nothing has changed but time.
And time has changed nothing.

To Sadhbh with Love

When these dark shadows pass
We will find you, forever young and beautiful
In the palm of God's hand,

Your infant eyes closed to the world,
Tiny fingers untainted by time,
Shapely feet that never knew the earth.

To Croíadh at Six Months

Halfway through your spoon-feed,
When you are lost in that faraway look,
That astray-with-angels look,
I fancy you have flashed back
To pre-conception – pure spirit
Considering future parents.

Quick as a blink, you are back
To your chosen ones,
Mouth open for an airborne spoonful
Gliding down to your airport.

A Glimpse of My Father

Long after his passing,
My father's gabardine overcoat
Remained hanging in the scullery –
Hook-bound wrinkles
Deepening with the passing of time.

My mother never moved it:
A mantle for her memories,
A shelter for his spirit,
A friendly shadow lingering.

Dabble Day

in memory of my mother

"We'll have good drying today," you'd say,
Your weather-eye reading the clouds;
"A good day for the *dabble*" –
A baby word you mothered for us.

Steaming sink of kettled water
Rich with *Rinso,*
Expanding bubbles, greedy for air,
Blinking back to nothingness.

In this symphony of suds
You baptised the sweat-stained garments
Of our daily labours –
Legacy of Adam's fall.

Your strong foam-sleeved arms
Restoring shirt and sheet
To Sunday grace
In the forgiving water;

Humid air surrendering to scullery walls,
Condensation indulging in its own calligraphy
As you rinsed and wrung
To clothesline readiness.

A mouthful of clothespegs, your third hand,
You wrestled with pneumatic ghosts,
Bulging and billowing shirt sleeve and trouser leg,
Invisible air-people claiming squatter's rights.

"They'll be dry in no time," you'd say,
Proud of your weather forecast,
Pleased with your *dabble day*.

In the fullness of time
You'd surrender to the twin-tub,
And *dabble*
Would be washed from your vocabulary.

Seventh Anniversary

Seven orbits round the sun
Without you,
For you're no longer tethered
To dimensions.

At ease with angels,
You smile at the limits
We place
On God's imagination.

Soul Search

I found the graveyard,
But I cannot find the grave.
I'm a small boat on an ocean, drifting.

Small comfort that this is your ocean
When I cannot find the shore
Where your voyage ended,
Your final moorings, where they lowered you
For the long sleep.

I brought these flowers for you.
I could leave them at the gate
And you would know that they were yours.
I could whisper to you from there
And you would hear me.
But the urge is strong
To see your name in stone
And touch your clay.

Twilight falls; farewell, dear friend.
Another shoreline beckons,
And my boat must sail.

Timeless Clay

And I leaned forward
As far as gravity would allow,
And peeped over the edge,
Down into the deep dark depths
Of my mother's freshly opened grave.

It was a score of years
Since this same clay received
My father's remains.

I was looking for some tangible
Sign of him – a lock of hair,
A rosary bead, perhaps.
But nothing –
Nothing, save the tarnished,
Mud-stained fragment
Of the brass plate
Which bore his final statistics:

PATRICK SHEAHAN
DIED 30th SEPTEMBER 1975
AGED 69 YEARS

And now it was my mother's turn
To enter the world of numbers
And timeless clay,
And again become one
With my father.

The Turf Cutter

Purple-tufted, mossy underlay,
Ancient carpet of the bog,
Crowning banks of fossil fuel,
Fire for winter's hearth.

Corrugated-iron shed,
Yawn of creaking, unlocked door
Awakens rusting tools
From idle slumber.

Taut line pegged
Parallel to bank's edge
Sets the target
For winter-warming harvest.

Rusty bluntness
Rasped to steely gleam.
Heathery carpet sliced back,
Ready for my father's *sleán*

To cut through a millennium
Of growth and decay, releasing
To a new generation the energy
Of forgotten forests and ancient suns.

Dreamtime

in memory of my mother

By flickering glow of twilight embers
You doze off mid-sentence,
Suspending me in a moment
That holds you forever.

In this intimate silence
Your aura ripples out
To encircle me.

I breathe in your soul,
Familiar features,
Stray wisps of silver,
Fire-lit glint of glasses.

I halt the hands of time,
Hush the whisper of settling embers,
Frame the room and store it all away,
Loathe to lose this hallowed moment.

When silence claims your space
This moment will unfold
To rekindle the flame,
And spirit you back
To your unfinished tale.

Woodsman

Your final earthly enclosure:
This long wooden box
Was once a living tree
That bowed to you in the forest,

Casting a cold dark shadow
Across your path –
A sigh of leafy air
Pre-ghosting your final breath.

And now your lifelines converge
In this twinned finality,
Your destinies closed forever
In familiar clay.

Sweepings of the Workshop

Art & Craft

The Chimney Sweep

A spread of old newspapers around the hearth,
And we knew he was expected. From early morning
We'd be on the lookout – black
As an engine driver, white-eyed under a sooty cap,
Stiff-bristled brushes strapped to the crossbar of the bike,
Ready for battle with the flue-lined waste
Of winter fires. *Mammy, the chimney sweep is here!*

"Ah! That was a hardy winter, Mam.
It'll be a tough job this time –" (An early hint
For a bigger tip.) "I see you're ready for me;
You can't bate the ould newspapers."

A soot-stained cloth with a hole in the middle
To mask the opening, and the black puppeteer
Was ready to perform. Up into the unknown
Went the first bristled head, and we watched, mesmerised,
As the hungry flue gobbled up one rod after another.

Coaxing it round an awkward bend,
He'd close his eyes, plotting the course in his head
Like a surgeon operating on a hidden organ.
Then with a subtle twist, he'd grunt it free.
"Must be the foreign coal," he'd mutter to himself.

"Should be coming out soon."
And we'd run outside and look up.
It's coming out! – the bristles vibrating with freedom,
The black puppet nodding in the dazzling daylight.

Behan's 'Children of Lir'

for John Behan, Master Sculptor

A spell from a legend,
Spirited into bronze.

Children of Lir, ill-fated by Aoife,
Moulded and cast
In mid-metamorphosis;

Guided by Behan's
Whimsical line and curve,
Fledgling wings
Strain towards weightlessness.

Half-earthling, half-swan;
Fionnuala, Fiachra, Aodh and Conn,
Hover forever between worlds.

Wood Carver

for Terry O'Brien, Master Carver

Leather-aproned, forest-perfumed,
Your knowing touch
Reads the promise of grain.

Percussion of mallet on chisel
Modulates from woodpecker fury
To tentative tap.

With eyes half closed,
You compare emerging profile
With imagined blueprint.

Balancing impulse with restraint,
You fine-tune features into focus,
A tunesmith

Lending grace notes to an air.

Wood Shavings

From the mouth of the plane,
Spring-like, somersaulting
Into a daring dangle,
You break loose
And spiral to the floor.

I pick you up, uncoil a curl,
And smell the ancient perfume
Kept secret until now.

The Solidity of Matter

i.m. Dick McCann, teacher

When you questioned the solidity of matter,
I postponed the crossing of a bridge;
When you marvelled at the uplift of a wing,
I flew with you unafraid.

When you were lost in the night sky,
I lured you back from a distant star.
Now I wander in a wasteland,
Bearing the weight of your absence.

When clocks have stopped,
And time surrenders to eternity,
You will rise to a new awareness
And drink from the fountain of knowledge,

The Fiddle Maker's Workshop

for Elfi Rautmann and Joseph Boasson

These workshop walls keep watch
On banks of time, secure in planks
Of ancient spruce and maple –
Saved and seasoned for bellies and backs
Of future fiddles.

In this peaceful place
Where timber talks and the master listens,
The wonder of a fiddle unfolds –
From the delicate spiral of the scroll
To the tail-piece that bears
All tension without complaint.

On workbench, wall and windowsill,
Traditional tools abound
To cut, carve, shape, drill,
Clamp and glue a family of wood
To live in harmony.

When all is set and settled,
Pernambuco bow and a swish
Of horse-hair whisper down
Through bridge and sound-post,
Waking memories of birdsong
In trees of an ancient forest.

Sweepings of the Workshop

Discarded debris of music;
Off-cuts, shavings, sawdust.

Gougings that gave contour
To back and belly.

F-hole cut-outs that liberate
The voice of a fiddle.

Unsung heroes –

Martyrs who fell
That angels might fly.

Signatures in Air

Times & Places

The Monthly Clip

Mirrored space
Strewn with *Star* and *Sun;*
Page Three and Saturday Sport
Well-thumbed.

Aproned host
Idly snipping the air;
Master of trivia
Addressing global issues:

D'ya know what I'm going to tell ya?
That NAMA lark'll have
The country knackered
When it's them bleedin' banks
Should be gettin' the hammer, not us …

Next please!

Juniors, shorn and shaped
By number,
Teenage fashion
De-skilling the trade!

Seniors, reassured by
Rhythmic snick of scissors;
Conjured flick of comb;
Rug of piebald clippings …

Yer talkin' about the Bono fella –
I'll give him one thing: he's a bleedin' good crooner,
But he shouldn't be pokin' his nose

Into G8 summits – out of his depth he is.
Should stick to chantin' with UB40
Or whoever they are!

Next please!

Caped with toreador flourish,
I'm beckoned to the chat-show chair
To co-star in mirrored dialogue.

He eyes my fleece.
I anticipate his opening line:
General tidy – the usual?

Out of Bounds

Fenced in. Out of bounds.
This silent land remembering
Summers of travellers,
With horse-drawn caravans,
Fashioning wares of tin.
Mending pots and pans.

Settled with us awhile,
Their lives touching ours
With colour – raggle-taggle
Menagerie – horses, goats, dogs
And a trail of ragged children.

Nutshell-cosiness of caravans –
Their private domain
Of make-shiftedness,
Economy of space,
Artefacts of tin,
Brass, and mirror
Reflecting the glow of the
Pot-bellied stove within.
Hunger-lines
Written on older faces,
Happy-go-lucky in their
Come-day, go-day …

Until suddenly one day …

Gone.

The lure of the open road too strong,
Spirited off to faraway hills
And greener pastures,
I followed them at a safe distance
In my boyhood's mind.

The age of plastic took its toll.
Tin smiths redundant –
Their craft no longer needed,
Thrown to the mercy of the dole.

Others drawn to scrapping cars
And selling parts –
Many an urban wasteland
Wears the scar.

This haunted land still dreaming …
Out of bounds … remembering,
Guarded now by jagged rocks and boulders:
"Travellers: move on."

Countdown

The night is alive with expectation,
The ghost of Janus climbs the belfry tower,
Friend and stranger bond in jubilation,
In chorused countdown to the midnight hour.

Cacophony of church bells raucous ringing,
Boisterous backfire bang of burst balloon,
Uncharted flight of cork from champagne popping,
A new year storming in, the old marooned.

The fanfare ends, we face a fresh beginning,
Old resolutions aired, retuned, re-sung,
We raise the odds, and hope for better innings,
Then climb again to reach the final rung,

Janus from the belfry tower descending,
Faces the beginning and the ending.

Silent Preacher

for Father Liam Hickey

Computer keyboard, your pulpit now;
Words of God, beneath your fingers;
Humble mouse in waiting,

No tumultuous gathering,
No spectacle of loaves and fishes,
Just you, speeding the Word

To gain the inbox of a soul.

Confession

I kneel at the grille
In the dark confessional,
Exposing my soul,

Part sinner, part saint,
A conflict of clay and wings,
Heaven-bound, hell-bent.

Connemara

Stone-clad, rock-strewn, barren landscape
Facing western sea and sky,
Windswept bogland, lake and rock-pool,
Shifting cloud and lambent light.

Yellow furze and purple heather,
Mantle of ever-changing hue,
Mountain palettes of green and brown
Challenging art to match your mood.

Cradling still your ancient culture,
Haunting sound of Gaelic tongue
Hovering on the twilight air,
Your lonely tunes and *sean-nós* song.

Aloof and proud, and yet alluring,
Cold of stone yet warm of heart,
Native talk with new tones blending,
Embracing change, yet worlds apart.

Trom agus Éadrom

Ag gabháil dom siar trí Bhinn Éadair,
Mo chosa go trom le gaineamh fliuch
'S mo smaointe comh héadrom leis an aer.

Na báid ag filleadh ón oíche
Go trom san uisce le gabháil éisc,
'S na faoileáin ag fáinneáil ós cionn
Chomh héadrom le mo smaointe.

*

And I going back through Howth,
My feet heavy with wet sand,
And my thoughts as light as the air.

The boats returning from the night,
Heavy in the water with the catch,
And the seagulls circling overhead,
As light as my thoughts.

Sunflowers

On slender stalks
You swivel from east to west
To follow the sun.

Do you unwind at night
Or wait till dawn
To face east again?

When the world is asleep
Do you lift your heads
To admire the moon?

Autumn

Autumn arrived in my garden this morning.
An orphaned leaf severed its bond with summer
And challenged the wind to a giddy waltz.

A lament keened its way through
Thinning branches, sighing for
The passing of the season.

Evening came shuffling in
On sandpaper soles, scattering
The crinkled pages of summer.

Tomorrow's wind will swirl the wizened
Waltzers into reckless pirouettes, to play
Catch Me If You Can with my garden rake.

Wheatfield Table

Arts Day, Wheatfield Prison, 26th June, 2007

I miss the wind and rain
And song-birds
That imbued my grain
With a latent gift.
Had fate been kind
I might have given voice
To strings or woodwind,
But I fell from grace
And the music died.

At night, I share your silence
When thoughts take flight
And pass between these bars;
When spirits soar and stray
Among the stars,
To return at dawn
To our prison cell.

Spare a thought for me,
Your Wheatfield table:
I too had another life.

Tree Seasons

Blossomed in Spring
Blessed in Summer
Bowed in Autumn
Bare in Winter

Stereo Tracks

From a speeding train
Telegraph poles are bar lines
Between sagging staves.

Perching birds are notes
Writing melody on wire –
Rhythm from the tracks.

Signature

The ploughman leaves his trace on field and furrow.
The sculptor's mark is etched in chiselled stone.
With sheaves of gold, the thatcher's name is written.
In rings of clay, the potter's name is known.

When day is done, and evening firelight beckons,
When tradesmen all are free from toil and care,
I linger in the shadows with my fiddle,
And softly leave my signature in air.

ABOUT THE AUTHOR

John Sheahan is one of Ireland's best known musicians. Born in Dublin in 1939, he was a member of *The Dubliners* from 1964 to 2012. He has played with musicians the world over and has guested on numerous folk, traditional and rock recordings. His own compositions, among them *The Marino Waltz* and *Autumn in Paris,* have become essential elements of the Irish musical repertoire. In 2013 he was conferred with an honorary doctorate in music from Trinity College, Dublin. In 2014 the television documentary *John Sheahan – A Dubliner* received two IFTA awards.